ALL THE HORSES THAT HE'D RODE

Preserving & Sharing Life In The West

A Collection of ORIGINAL PAINTINGS by DARYL POULIN
&
POETIC INTERPRETATIONS by CHARLIE HUNT

Dageforde Publishing, Inc.
Crete, Nebraska

ISBN 1-886225-69-9

Library of Congress Control Number: 2001092293

Cover Painting by Daryl Poulin

Cover design by Angie Johnson

DAGEFORDE
Publishing, inc.

Dageforde Publishing, Inc.
128 East 13th Street
Crete, Nebraska 68333-2235
Ph: (402) 826-2059 FAX: (402) 826-4059
email: info@dageforde.com

Visit our website: www.dageforde.com

Printed in the United States of America
10   9   8   7   6   5   4   3   2   1

Contents

What readers are saying...

Daryl Poulin and Charlie Hunt have masterfully captured the spirit and the essence of life in the West. In picture and verse, **All The Horses That He'd Rode** *paints a vivid portrait of our great western heritage.*

South Dakota Congressman, John Thune

Theodore Roosevelt said, 'Ours was the glory of work and the joy of living.' This marvelous book offers us not only glory and joy, but warmth, love, humor, beauty and a delicious taste of our Western hereitage. A wonder-filled blend of paint and poetry—thanks to Daryl Poulin and Charlie Hunt.

Harold Schafer, President and Founder of Gold Seal Co., Founder of Theodore Roosevelt Medora Foundation, Former President of National Cowboy Hall of Fame, Winner of Horatio Alger Award and North Dakota's highest honor—The Theodore Roosevelt Rough Rider Award.

All The Horses That He'd Rode *is a wonderfully written, beautifully illustrated new book of Charlie Hunt's poetry combined with Daryl Poulin's original paintings. Charlie presents us with a clear-eyed, straight shooter's look at life's trials and trails, cowdogs, and cavvy quitters. Those of us who know Charlie would have expected no less.*

Mike Logan, Helena, MT, photographer, author of *Ranchin' Is, Bronc to Breakfast, Men of the Open Range, Laugh Kills Lonesome*

In verse and vivid paintings, Charlie Hunt and Daryl Poulin evoke the spirit of the West its men, its horses, its mountains, and its God.

Elmer Kelton, San Angelo, TX, author of *The Day It Never Rained, Good Old Boys*, and many others

Never in all my years of living and enjoying the Art and Poetry of the West have I seen anything better than the work of these two great artists. The beautiful way of expressing the life of the WEST and the horses he rode is outstanding. Complimenting the paintings in no uncertain terms is the poetry by Charlie Hunt to tell the story of the painting. In spite of the years of life he has lead, Charlie always comes through to keep the Western life as we know it alive. I hope all of you have the same privilege some day to know this man as we have and realize he is the best as a friend as well as a poet.

John Hutson, professional rodeo announcer and former president of NHSRA

The painter and the poet depict the historic West with brilliant pictures and words.

Virginia Driving Hawk Sneve, author of *The Trickster and the Troll, Grandpa Was A Cowboy and An Indian*, Recipient of the National Endowment for the Humanities medal for promoting Native American Culture in her teaching

Just opening the cover of **All the Horses That He'd Rode** *releases sage-scented prairie breezes. The authentic colorful cowboy images from the brushes of Daryl Poulin take on heart and soul through the skillfully written interpretations of true cowboy Charlie Hunt. If you're a cowboy, you'll find truth in the illustrations and the words that encapsulate the rhythms of the cowboy's very soul.*

Rhonda Sedwick Stearns, Author of Prairie Trails of Miz Mac, Sky Trails, Trails of a Wanderer, and Mush Creek Musings

I think it would be fair to say Charlie Hunt outdid himself. The pictures are postcard perfect and Charlie's poems are their equal. It's a hard combination to beat. (PS: The last verse of "Freedom" is a standout.)

Baxter Black, Benson, AZ, author, humorist, veterinarian, cowboy, and cowboy poet

My pal Charlie Hunt and his colleague Daryl Poulin go together like sourdough biscuits and beans. Their collaboration on this worthy project is like a rare gem...something you don't see often! Their combined talents and love of the Great American West comes through like a "Blue Norther" in the Texas Panhandle. This is one book you'll be proud to add to your collection.

Jim Gough, Liberty Hills, TX, actor, guitar "picker," proud fourth generation Texan

I liked the poems and paintings very much. Good horses and sturdy riders are poetry in motion and fit subjects for an artist's canvas. The stellar collaboration of poet Charlie Hunt and artist Daryl Poulin treats readers to both. Saddle up!

B. Byron Price, Cody, WY, Executive Director of Buffalo Bill Historical Center

Good ballads paint a picture in the mind of the reader. Charlie Hunt writes good pictures of the cowboy and the Indian. His love of the land and its people is evident and although Daryl Poulin's exceptional paintings tell the story in vivid color, Charlie's poems took me there on their own. Good reading, Charlie, and great pictures, Daryl. Thanks for the trip and all the horses that you've rode.

Red Steagall, Ft. Worth, TX, singer, songwriter, Author of *Ride for the Brand*, and poem, "For Freckles Brown," Official Cowboy Poet of the state of Texas

Charlie Hunt is loved and recognized as an over-achiever who has done it all. He daily lives his cowboy heritage of honor, faith, humor, and dedication to God and His creation. This book **All the Horses That He'd Rode** *beautifully reflects the heart of this very special man of the West as Daryl Poulin reflects it in his paintings.*

Vivian Spencer Cannon, Lindale, TX, author, columnist, and cowboy poet

What a wonderful idea for a book-taking the paintings of Daryl Poulin and pairing them with a poem written for it by Charlie Hunt. And I'm not just saying this because both of you are so closely associated with the Artist Ride, or that I happen to appear in one of the paintings! Good luck partners!

Jim Hatzell, Rapid City, SD, Fiddler's Green Studio, artist, actor, and artist ride honcho

Pictures and words, painted and written in a way that could only come from men who understand the cowboy way of life. What a fantastic production by two who've been there. I've shared a lot of coffee with Charlie at 4:30 in the morning on cattle drives and wagon trains and I've shared many a late night campfire with Daryl. A sincere thanks for sharing your incredible talents with the rest of us and preserving a way of life for generations to come.

Kyle Evans, Rodeo contract performer and South Dakota Centennial Troubadour

A winning combination! Words by Cowboy Poet Charlie Hunt who, as a rancher himself, writes with depth and understanding possible only to one who "has been there and done that." Paintings by outstanding Western artist Daryl Poulin. The result— a beautiful book, an evocative book, a treasure for anyone's library.

Rex Alan Smith, author, *Moon of Popping Trees, The Carving of Meeting Rushmore, One Last Look*

Acknowledgments

*T*his book is dedicated to the people—red, white, black, brown, and yellow—who made this country what it was and what it is, and especially to those who built and are still building and preserving the West.

We also want to express our appreciation for our wives: Debbie Poulin and Glorine Hunt. Without their help, their belief, their encouragement, their patience and their willingness to cosign notes, this book would not have been.

And to those cowboys and Indians who have shared their history and their presence in keeping alive the West, we'll be eternally grateful as we will to those who were so gracious in their words on the dust jacket. A special note of appreciation to the late Bonnie Colleen Hunt Briest who taught us much about preparing a manuscript for the publisher, and to the people who helped put this one together—Tom and Kelly Leonard and Rocky Kindred—who spent countless hours straightening out the messes we made on the computer so it could go to the publisher. And to Linda Dageforde and her people at Dageforde Publishing who not only took a chance on us when most publishers were quick to say, "We don't do inside color. It's too expensive." Not only were they good, they were tremendous to work with as they guided us.

Daryl Poulin and Charlie Hunt

All The Horses That He'd Rode

His hat was stained an' battered.
His stirrups were wooden bows.
The inside of his chaps showed miles of wear.
His eyes were sharp and sparkly
As he gazed across the plains.
His Stetson topped the silver in his hair.

His Paint horse close beside him
Nudged his head against his arm.
For years this pair had lived the cowboy way.
From sun-up ev'ry mornin'
When they rode out through the gate
They had counted on each other through the day.

It had been 'most sixty summers
Since his dad had bought the place.
Some thirty summers since his dad had died.
Lookin' out across the prairie
Mem'ries raced across his mind
An' he got a funny feelin' deep inside.

It was such an empty feelin'
It brought a mist into his eyes.
But he also had a calmin' sense of pride.
He an' Paint had put their years in.
He an' Paint both needed rest.
He an' Paint both knew this was their final ride.

All his horses had been pardners.
Each was more than just a tool.
When each grew old another he would find,
But when each horse went to pasture
An' another took his place
Each one became a mem'ry in his mind.

Tomorrow his son takes over.
Tomorrow he moves to town.
Another generation now would bear the load.
An' he thought about the grandsons
Who would someday run this place,
An' he thought of all the horses that he'd rode.

All The Horses That He'd Rode

High on a Horse

There's somethin' 'bout sittin' on top of a horse
That makes you feel like a king.
A Hamley or Veach a' spreadin' your knees
Brings a joy nothin' else can bring.

Maybe you're cuttin' a cow from the herd,
Or maybe you're ropin' a calf,
Or maybe you're ridin' beyond the next hill—
Nothin' can touch it, not half!

You're out in the open beneath God's big sky.
Your body's a part of your steed.
Your cares melt away an' joy fills your heart—
What more could anyone need?

City folks brag on their Mustangs an' Colts,
Their Pintos, made of steel, of course,
But no car can ever give you the feelin'
You'll get when you're sittin' on top of your horse.

High on a Horse

Wet Saddle Blankets

A saddle blanket's just a smelly ol' rug
To city folks when they visit a ranch.
An' their sour smell in the warm summertime
Can make a city girl blanch.

It comes between the horse an' the saddle
An' keeps sore spots off of his back.
An' it also protects the good sheepskin
Saddlemakers use for linin' the kack.

Laundromat owners sure hate 'em—
Say they really mess up their machine.
So a real cowboy lets 'em soak in a creek
Held by rocks until they come clean.

But a Navaho blanket's a treasure,
That costs many dollars, of course,
An' it takes a heap of wet blankets
To turn a cayuse into a horse.

Wet Saddle Blankets

Before the Wire

It was hot driving down through the bottoms today.
　　　The flies was 'most coverin' the cows.
It was kinda like back home in Texas again
　　　An' this grass ain't been touched by the plows.

We crossed the Platte River 'fore sundown last night.
　　　An' camped the cows on this side.
As the sun started climbin' over the rim
　　　We'd moved 'most a mile on this ride.

The sun overhead says the day is half gone.
　　　The shadows are under the horse.
By sundown this evenin' when the chuckwagon parks
　　　We'll be seven more miles on our course.

It's a glorious drive that our outfit is on.
　　　Free of rustlers, flood and range fire.
We know that we're drivin' the last of the herds
　　　Before they start stringin' barb wire.

So we sit here together an' share the canteen.
　　　We're close to Wyomin' at last.
We're a part of the his'try that made this land great
　　　For these drives are now things of the past.

Before the Wire

Waste — Good!

There's a feast at the camp of Lakota.
The hunt was a good one today.
The women have butchered and cooked it.
We've invited our *teospa ye*.

Our extended family will join us.
At the fire we'll share of our gain
And the *nagt*—the spirit of *tatanka*
Will rejoice he did not die in vain.

We three have carried the message.
And asked our friends to come share.
It is the good way of the Lakota.
Waste. It is good that we care.

The Lakota words:
Teospa ye—the extended family
Nagt—ghost or spirit
Tatanka—the male buffalo
Waste (wash TAY)—It is good

Waste — Good!

White Boots

When Grandad hung his brand on this place
There wasn't no fences nowhere.
He said, "This is my brand
An' these are my cows
An' we'll graze from right here to right there.

An' a hundred years are somehow begun
Where my brand an' my cattle will always be run
  For this is my grass
  An' centuries will pass
For my son an' the sons of my son!"

Well, I'm not the last to carry the brand,
Though I've not any sons for the land.
  Now this daughter you're seein'
  May be judged as a queen,
At home we just call her "a hand."

She's at home in the saddle or back of the chutes.
She's sound as can be when it comes to her roots.
  She's at home in the mud
  The manure and blood
But she's shore lookin' sharp in white boots.

White Boots

Snoball

The cowboys all like Snoball.
He's a bareback horse deluxe
'Cause half of their score is counted
On the way that their pony bucks.

If you're able to ride all eight seconds
You'll be known as one of the few
Who picked up their check at the window
Because of this horse that you drew.

An' the pickup men find their job's easy
'Cause ol' Snoball keeps buckin' so rank
They don't have to rescue the cowboy—
He's gone! They just have to pull flank.

Snoball

Smellin' the Wild Ones

Lookit' ol' TeeVer, standin' there tense.
He hears 'em off up the canyon today.
That ol' Paint stud that got away from John Lee
Is takin' his females to play.

The blood of the ages runs thru TeeVer's veins.
The challenge of battle is near.
The call of the wild reaches into his heart
An' it sometimes fills me with fear

'Cause that two-rail corral ain't enough for a stud,
An' a stall ain't no place for a horse,
But he's suckin' in wind to challenge that Paint
To come an' do battle, of course.

The smell of that saddle reminds him of me
An' he slows to the sound of my voice
An' I softly say, "Steady, ol' boy!"
As I watch him relax, I rejoice.

But no matter how gentle, no matter how old,
A horse is still part of the wild
An' God's great creation has such a strong call
To a stallion—He's jist like this child.

We both hate the thought of bein' confined.
We both search the ends of the earth.
Ol' TeeVer an' me, we're two of a kind
An' we've both been that way since our birth.

Smellin' the Wild Ones

17

Thunder on the Rimrock

That ol' brindle longhorn's still watching me.
It's a game we've been playin' last hour.
Since I moved her out of that plum thicket she liked
She's progressively been gettin' more sour.

We're movin' the herd from their high summer range
An' we're takin' 'em down by the crick,
But that bunch-quittin' mossy-horn Longhorn right there
Is sure tryin' to figure a trick.

Ev'ry time that we've come to a tree or a draw
She's hidden or broke into a run,
But this ol' Jigger horse ain't even broke sweat—
That ol' Longhorn is his kind of fun.

I don't blame her a lot, though I wish she would quit,
For the Rimrock's a place of its own,
An' I hate to see us gath'rin' the herd
For it means winter's changin' our home.

The thunder of summer is the lightnin's own tune
That plays out in each summer night's storm,
But the thunder of hooves as the herd makes its run
Is the reason a cowboy was born.

Yes, the cow an' the horse an' the cowboy himself
Know that winter must follow the fall.
An' when it turns spring we'll climb the Rimrock again
For the Rimrock is home to us all.

Thunder on the Rimrock

Anniversary Present

She's been doin' her share of hintin'—
Like she does most ev'ry year—
An' I pretend to ignore it
An' answer her with a "Yes, dear."

She talks about the day we was married—
Thinks interested I'm not.
She talks about clothes in the catalogue.
I talk about clothes that she's got.

There's a cake mix out on the counter.
It's been there most of three days.
I ask her, "Why don't you bake us some bread?
I sure like the smell of its raise."

I know that she thinks I forgot it,
But, Lordy, I love her a lot.
She can buy all the fancy clothes that she wants.
I'll buy her the present I got.

This red dun will treat her plumb gentle.
He's a horse she can ride without fear.
This evenin' I'll saddle my horse an' hers
An' say, "I'd shore like your company, dear."

Let's go for a ride in the moonlight.
Put some romantic back in our life.
So, "Happy Anniversary, Darlin'—
I'm sure proud to call you my wife."

Anniversary Present

All American

Women, they say, are the weaker sex
While cowboys are macho an' rough.
Rodeo is a sport made for men—
Men who are athletic an' tough.

But these girls are all rodeo queens.
All four of them look better than boys.
They've all competed in contests for queens
Testing knowledge an' speakin' an' poise.

They've demonstrated their best horsemanship
In saddle an' down on the ground.
They prob'ly competed in runnin' the barrels—
Made appearances all over town.

Tonight with pride they will carry the flags
Of the sponsors, their land, rodeo.
They're all part of the American West
An' the best lookin' part of the show.

So we'll tip our Resistols to each of these girls.
As they ride, we'll salute with a cheer.
They're part of the rodeo, part of the West,
They're All-American Queens without peer.

All American

Cold Wind A'blowin'

Lord, it was shore cold this mornin'.
The blanket got stiff overnight.
I warmed up the bit 'fore he took it
An' pulled both the cinches up tight.

But Jackson still had a hump in his back
So I tracked him around for a spell,
Then rode out the crowhops before we lined out
An' went off to check on the well.

The tank sure was froze an' the windmill almost.
With my axe I broke out the ice.
The beef cows went bumpin' an' pushin' around
An' didn't need no advice.

Tonight my chaps are all stiff, my ears are plumb
numb.
My fingers and toes are like sticks.
The steel of my spurs has run ice through my
heels
An' my nose mostly runs like a crick.

Now we're back at the gate, Jackson an' me,
The afternoon sun almost set.
But we've done us the job we're created to do
An' we ain't complainin' as yet

'Cause some hay an' some grain an' a brisk rubbin'
down
Will have Jackson enjoyin' his rest,
While some beans an' some beef, cooked on a
wood fire,
Will finish my day with the best.

Maybe tomorrow the clouds will be gone.
Maybe the sun will shine through.
Maybe the wind will stop blowin' so hard
An' our job will be easy to do.

But it don't make much diff'rence.
We'll do it both ways,
'Cause it's the job we've elected to do.
We'll keep those cows healthy an' growing' an'
fed
'Til they become top beef for someone like you.

Cold Wind A'blowin'

Mornin' Coffee

Here, have a cup o' coffee, pard,
  It'll start your day out right.
It's the thing I'm needin' each mornin'
  To drive away the dark night.

Cookin' on a campfire or wood stove
  Heat your water up to a boil.
Jist use my good recipe, ol' pard,
  It's shore mighty hard to spoil.

Take somebody's good ol' work sock
  Before they git out of bed.
Tie a knot to close the holes in the toes.
Use baling twine instead of your thread.

The tin cup separates the real men
From those fuzzy-chinned young boys
Who, when the hot cup hits their lips,
  Bring forth a passel of noise.

There's a secret to drinkin' our coffee, pard.
  Slop some coffee 'cross the hot rim.
It cools the cup where it meets with the lips
  But still leaves the hot flavor within.

There, now, the day's lookin' better.
  We've still got a' plenty to do,
But that ol' pot o' good mornin' coffee
Will sure see this ol' cowboy through.

Mornin' Coffee

27

Looking for an Answer

The *wasicu* came across the big river.
The treaty they made, they have broken.
It's always that way when they sign the white page
Buying our land for a token.

The Seven Council Fires of the Lakota
The *ocheli shakowin* are kindled again.
Anag Ite and *tokahe* gave direction
To be brave—*walitakya*—be men!

The *uncis*—grandmothers—remember
When the buffalo covered the land.
Now the *Pahin* with his quills is our eating.
It's time that we Sioux take a stand.

The *Paha Sapa*—the Black Hills—are so sacred
Wasicu should not even trod.
Our barefooted ponies make small tracks
Unlike the ponies of whites which are shod.

The *wasicu* are enemy—*toka*.
Our life they would bring to an end.
How can we make them our family—
Tiospa ye—our *kola*—our friend?

The Lakota words:
Ocheli Shackowin—the council fires of the seven bands of Lakota, a part of the
  Sioux nation
Uncis—grandmothers
Wasicu—the white man
Anag Ite—the double faced woman of the Lakota creation story
Walitakya—to be brave
Pahin—the porcupine
Paha Sapa—the Black Hills
Tokahe—the first man
Tiospa ye—the extended family
Toka—enemy
Kola—friend

Looking for an Answer

Bringin' in the Cavvy

Lookit' ol' Hercules, there in the lead,
He's orn'ry an' sure on the fight.
He's the only one in the cavvy this year
That you have to watch for his bite.

Ol' Paint's gettin' old and set in his ways,
But at cuttin' he's one of the best.
It's when you get on him you have to be set
'Cause he'll hump up just like the rest.

An' Tony, the bay, sure is good with a rope.
He'll drag calves to the fire all day,
But that short coupled rascal will jar loose your bones
'Til you'll swear he eats steel 'stead of hay.

An' Possum, in back, is shore gonna buck
When you crawl in the saddle come morn'.
The man who stays on him can brag jist a bit...
The others regret he was born.

These four are bunch quitters if they get the chance.
The three of us had us a fight
To bring 'em on down to the cavvy today.
I jist hope we don't lose 'em tonight

'Cause each has his faults, like most folks we know,
An' each has a trait that we need.
So this wild ride was worth it! They're back!
An' that's part of a good cowboy's creed.

Bringin' in the Cavvy

Northern Plains Cowboy

His hair is mostly gray or gone.
His stirrups are gettin' higher.
His horses all seem taller now
An' the gates have stiffer wire.

But the cow still needs a cowboy
Like a steamship needs a crew.
Born maybe 50 years too late
He'll still do what cowboys do.

In the California mountains
Or the wild Oyahee range
Or the Gulf Coast down in Texas
The cowboy ain't so strange.

His hats an' boots may differ
An' his chaps be diff'rent length
But the man is still a cowboy
When he shows his inner strength…

That don't let him take advantage
Of someone down and out—
An' don't let him start a braggin'—
He'll just get by without

'Cause it's his own horse he saddles
An' no quarter's asked or given.
He's just proud to be a cowboy
In the West—right close to Heaven.

Northern Plains Cowboy

33

She Speaks Softly

Silently she watches the men with their paint
As each checks his arrows and bow.
Her heart splits between her fears and her pride
As the warriors prepare for the Crow.

Last night the Crow had raided their herd.
And horses are missing today,
But Lakota warriors will go bring them back.
Soon they will be on their way.

She keeps her soft eyes from the one that she loves.
Her eyes she averts from their force.
In her heart there is mingling of her fear and her love
And She Speaks Softly of them to his horse.

She Speaks Softly

Return of the Stolen Ponies

Three sleeps have passed since the raid on their herd.
The Kangi (the Crow) had been quick.
For three days Lakota had followed their trail
To where they camped last night by a creek.

While the Crow ate and prepared for the night,
The Lakota had freshened their paint,
Patiently waiting 'til the Crow were asleep
And the light of the moon became faint.

The whispered Lakota words settled the herd
While they slipped a thong on their head.
With silent Sioux knives they disposed of their foe
And soon all of the Kangi were dead.

Hokahe! was their cry as they battled the foe.
Hokahe! echoed early and late.
Hokahe! swelled their throats as their knives did their job.
Hokahe! Waken Tanka is great!

The Nez Perce war horse, the big old Palouse,
On the prairie his kind are still few,
And every horse lost is a horse they lead back
For you don't steal a horse from the Sioux.

The Lakota words:
    Hokahe! (sometimes Huk hey!)—Let's go! Charge! A war cry
    Waken Tanka—the Great Spirit, the Creator

Return of the Stolen Ponies

37

Contemplatin' Cowboy

The brandin's done, the calves are weaned,
The cows are bawlin' loud.
The neighbors headed home jist now.
I'm all that's left of the crowd.

We neighbor out here together,
Each with a helpin' hand.
There ain't no pay for neighborin'.
That's jist how it is in this land.

I'm sittin' here watchin' the beef cows
An' list'nin' to the mother cows bawl.
The last truck's gone over the hilltop
There's jist me an' the wife, an' that's all.

In ranchin' we count on our neighbors
An' our neighbors can sure count on us.
Shucks, it's the way of life we was raised in.
We don't ever think twice or fuss.

I know it ain't that way in the cities.
You don't even know the next door.
You pull down your shades at a problem
An' don't get involved anymore.

But the cowboy way is a good one
For a man an' his kids an' his wife,
So I'll jist sit here for a minute
An' give thanks for the cowboy life.

Contemplatin' Cowboy

Warshirt

Listen, my brothers, to the sound of the guns!
Listen to the screams of the men!
Hurry, my brothers, or we will be late!
Come, ride to the battle again!

Yellow Hair came with the sound of the horn
Then ran away to the hill.
Hurry, my brothers, before it's too late—
Wait! Listen! The hilltop is still!

Warshirt

41

A million and a half Texas Longhorns went up the trail between 1867 and 1871—first to Kansas, then to Colorado, the Black Hills, Montana and the Chugwater area of Wyoming. The trail drive was long and dusty, dry and full of danger. It was a job for young men with a taste for adventure. Many went on to become successful ranchers. Others never made it to the end of the trail. Many days they saw a…

Horse Without a Rider

Jack was only 16 on that warm April day
Said that his home was too tame.
"I want to help drive those Longhorns up North.
West Texas Jack is my name."

After we'd gathered them cows from the bush
Jack worked at the old dipping vat.
Then we'd crossed the Red at the border.
The Canadian, Washita and Platte.

He saw the bright lights of Ogallala
Before we turned off to the West
An' that "Dodge City of the North" sure enough
Put a little more hair on his chest.

This dawn he went scouting for water
As we took the Chugwater Trail.
The responsibility was his an'
To find water he just couldn't fail.

We didn't start in to worry about him
Until after noon he's not back.
So Jim and I changed to fresh horses
An' went looking for West Texas Jack.

When we saw his ol' horse standing ground tied
We knew something shore had gone bad.
When we found Jack lying there on the ground
What a terrible moment we had.

Three arrows had pierced his young body.
His scalplock was missing complete.
His West Texas chaps were still on his legs
An' his West Texas boots on his feet.

We buried him there on the prairie he loved
Where the coyotes can sing him a song.
We put some rocks on top of his grave
But we didn't tarry too long.

When we get back to Texas sometime
We'll take his mother the saddle he rode.
And she'll see that horse without a rider
Is back a'runnin' with the herd.

There's many a handsome young rider
Buried 'longside of the trail.
Many a horse without a rider
Is proof of a similar tale.

Horse Without a Rider

What's It Take to Be a Cowboy?

What's it take to be a cowboy?
There's some things shore, of course.
If you're gonna be a cowboy
You need a saddle an' a horse,

A pair of chaps to save your legs,
A hat to save your face,
An' leather cuffs to save your arms
Ain't never out of place.

A working dog is shore a help
Your boots an' spurs are too,
But you're plumb put out of business
When your ol' horse throws a shoe.

If you've got a fencin' tool an' nails
In the pocket of your chaps
You can maybe make that ol' shoe tight
An' save a walk, perhaps.

None of these things make a cowboy.
It's a guts an' grins an' skill—
An' ability to do the job—
Jist watchin' Kyle's a thrill.

No, it ain't the clothes. It ain't the horse.
It shouldn't seem too strange.
It's a lifetime of workin' cattle
On a horse out on the range.

It's BlackJack chewin' prairie grass.
It's ol' Chip dog on guard.
But it's Kyle who's still the cowboy.
Horse an' dog are just his pards.

What's It Take to Be a Cowboy?

The Storm-Born Calf

The blizzard hit 'bout 10 AM—
I'd jist got into town.
The partsman hollered, "Charlie,
Your foreman's tracked you down."

Pickin' up the telephone
I heard Lee holler, "Come!
The cows are calvin' in this storm—
We'll be losin' ev'ry one!"

Headin' home, I saddled up
And fought out through the snow.
Ol' Doc hit drifts above his knees
But still that hoss would go.

When I reached a grove of trees
I found my work cut out.
Eighteen cows had dropped their
calves
An' couldn't get about.

Grabbin' sacks I wiped away
An' tried to dry each one
While dodgin' mother-cow attacks...
I sure was havin' fun.

Then I watched this Hereford cross
Lay down an' soon give birth.
The little calf arrived alright
But never touched the earth.

Steamin' hot, it hit the snow
An' ice formed on that calf.
Like a sled it slid down hill,
Givin' me a laugh.

In fifty feet it crossed a fence
By slidin' underneath.
I watched it slide on down the hill
With speed beyond belief

'Til finally it hit a tree.
Its slide came to a stop.
Mother cow's a'lookin' round
To find her new calf crop.

So down the hill I slid some, too,
To steamin' baby's side.
Picked it up an' started back—
Givin' calf a ride.

Laid it down to cross the fence...
Picked it up again...
Looked around for mother cow...
Couldn't find her. Then

Saw her headin' 'cross the draw
Another calf beside.
That fool cow had stole a calf
An' left her calf to die.

Picked up baby calf once more
An' held it in my arms.
No use to try to catch that cow—
I'd save the calf from harm.

Fightin' drifts, I reached ol' Doc.
Head down and legs a'straddle
I laid that calf across his neck
An' crawled up in the saddle.

Buckin' blizzard...headed home.
I'd shore surprise my spouse
When she got home from town
An' found a new calf in the
house.

When dried off calf was safe an'
warm
Within a rag-filled box
Beside the bathroom register
I changed my boots an' sox.

A little later wife came home
An' went to use the john.
I don't know what went through
her mind—
She never did let on,

But lookin' at her cowboy
With a gaze as soft as silk,
She went out in the kitchen
An' started mixin' milk.

The fam'ly ranch ain't just a job—
It's plumb a way of life.
An' we cowboys couldn't do it
Without our cowgirl wife.

46

The Storm-Born Calf

Guardians

Look, my brothers. Look!
Look to the place where the sun starts each day.
There is no sign of our people.
They are deep in the *Mako Sica*.

Look, my brothers. Look!
Look to the place where the sun goes to rest.
Here we four stand—stand for our people.
We stand on the edge of *Papa Sapa*.

Look, my brothers. Look!
Look where our women and our children are invisible.
Here we stand together to guard from the *Wasicu*.
Until the time when we shall be no more.

The Lakota words:
Mako Sica—the Badlands
Paha Sapa—the Black Hills
Wasicu—white people

Guardians

Sunfishin' Son of a Gun

There was frost on the blanket this mornin'
An' a hump in the back of ol' Turk.
He swelled up when I tightened the cinch
An' I kneed him and give him a jerk.

When my foot hit the stirrup he stood there
'Til I planted myself on his back,
Then he went to sunfishin' an' rollin' behind—
Tryin' to unload both me an' the kack.

'Cause the cold mountain air is a tonic
That starts a horse buckin' for fun.
But he'll settle down soon an' he'll work all day long,
That sunfishin' son-of-a-gun.

Sunfishin' Son of a Gun

Last One Buys the Drinks

We've got the herd bedded down two miles south of Dodge.
We've been a long time on the trail.
We've fought the dry drives an' we've fought us some floods.
We've gone without women or mail.

Tomorrow we drive to the pens in the town.
Tonight we're as wild as the Lynx.
We're three Texas cowboys a headin' for fun
An' the last cowboy there buys the drinks.

Last One Buys the Drinks

53

End of the Trail

We're rugged an' tough, we're wild and we're grand.
Each of us here's a ferocious top hand.
Look at our weapons. Look at our clothes.
Just how good we are, really, nobody knows.

We rode out of Texas and we're in Abilene.
This town is the wildest that we've ever seen.
There's whiskey an' women an' gamblin' for all.
What stories we'll tell when we get home this fall.

When we get home we'll shore brag of our fun.
They won't know we borrowed the clothes an' the gun.
This photographer said we're each handsome alone—
Together we three will impress them back home.

End of the Trail

Seven Buffalo

The prairie grass is long and brown.
The weather's growing cold.
There's fires in the tipis now.
It's a story centuries old.

The buffalo once roamed these plains
As far as eye could see
These seven now are all that's left
Of the buffalo that made us free.

Our tipis were made of their hide.
Their meat our bellies would fill.
The white man then came hunting hides—
Others shot just for the thrill.

Our food supply quickly was gone.
Our tipis soon wore out.
The reservation took their place.
They couldn't hear us shout,

"You steal from us our way of life!
We are not free to roam!"
Our freedom, like the buffalo,
Was traded for a home.

The white man stole the buffalo,
But still a greater theft
Was when our freedom disappeared.
Just seven buffalo are left.

Seven Buffalo

57

A Cowboy Day

When you come to the end of a cowboy day
An' your supper is scheduled soon,
An' you're hungrier than a grizzly bear
'Cause you didn't stop at noon...

When you know your supper's beans an' beef
Or wild game, if you kill it,
An' coffee hot as Hell's inside
An' bread fried in a skillet.

When the fiery hot of the afternoon
Gives way to the ev'nin's cold
An' the third mustang you've rode that day
No longer's actin' bold...

When your skin's all burned an' blistered
An' all your muscles hurt,
An' the night breeze is dehydratin'
Your soggy, sweat-soaked shirt...

When your reata's stretched its limit
From jerkin' down each calf,
An' your mouth is dry as cotton
An' you still can make a laugh...

When the spot the brandin' iron burned
Don't bother overmuch,
An' the gash the knife made when it slipped
Is still tender to the touch...

When they have to peel your saddle off
Where your behind meets the leather,
An' your spur strap's broke an' your shirt is tore
An' it looks like stormy weather...

When you know that near the midnight
You'll do two hours more
A'ridin' through the bedground
When you'd really rather snore...

When you've had this kind of day, my friend,
An' you still ain't feelin' glum,
You've had a cowboy day, ol' pard...
Go ahead an' swagger some!

A Cowboy Day

The Gathering Storm

There's a storm gathering now in the sky in the west.
It's soon coming near to the rim.
The wind in advance is blowing the grass
And the sun is growing more dim.

The horses are feeling the weather to come
As they turn their rumps to the hill.
The sky's turning black and the shadows are close—
Another storm brings warriors a thrill.

Wovoka, the Piute, his vision has told:
The buffalo—*pte*— will return.
And all of the *wasicu* will be gone from the land—
A dream for which we all yearn.

Kicking Bear tells of a shirt we can wear
That will turn all the bullets aside
As we drive all the white men far from our lands
And once again live with our pride.

The messenger comes to show us the way
To become of Messiah a part.
There's a storm gathering now in the sky in the west
And a storm's gathering now in our hearts.

When this storm is over and the white man is gone
The Lakota will again own the land.
Wovoka has spoken. We follow his lead—
We're proud to be part of his band.

The Lakota words:
   Wovoka—a Piute Indian whose vision was of the return of the buffalo
         would replace the white man on the earth
   Kicking Bear—a Lakota whose vision was of the bullet-proof Ghost Shirt
         Pte—the buffalo
         Wasicu—the white man

The Gathering Storm

The Getaway

The bank in that little ol' town that we hit
Looked easy when we chose it to crack.
A skinny young man was alone in the cage
An' a wizened ol' man in the back.

We waited 'til it was just closin' time
An' the last customer walked out the door.
We walked in together as the clock struck the hour
An' asked if they'd wait on one more.

With pistols in hand we braced the young man—
"Put all of your cash in this sack!
If you don't make a wrong move you'll live to be old—
We'll leave an' we'll never come back."

The young feller turned as white as a ghost.
He started to shake like a leaf.
He'd rather put all that he had in the sack
Than fall dead at the hand of a thief.

We should have been careful an' watched that ol' prune.
He was made out of gizzard an' grit.
He grabbed his ol' Greener an' started to shoot.
We grabbed the sack an' we split.

The extra horses we'd brought for our run
Are all that we've got in our hand.
We dropped the sack somewhere in the street
An' that's not at all what we'd planned.

We've learned us a lesson, just hope not too late.
We've found out that crime doesn't pay
An' old men are dangerous when they fight for the right
An' we're hoping we'll just get away!

The Getaway

63

Ghost of the Plains

A century it lay there, a part of the past.
I know I'd have missed if I'd been ridin' fast.
But the sun hit it right
So I noticed the white
An' the mem'ry forever will last.

Dismounting, I gently gave it a pull
An' I held the skull of a buffalo bull.
The sight was unreal
But it had such appeal
Overwhelming—an' so powerful.

The Paint horse just stood there so grand.
Then the brave gave a wave of his hand.
The statement he made,
As he started to fade,
Was "White man. Take care of my land!"

As this vision was beginning to fade
I put the skull where it had laid
In the eternal domain
Of this Ghost of the Plains
It was part of a debt still unpaid.

Ghost of the Plains

Fall Calves

Hey, ol' hoss...that rimrock's mighty pretty
Above them pines so green.
The aspen trees are bare today...
The wind has stripped 'em clean.

It's been a dandy summer
With rain enough this year
To keep our grass a'growin'
An' take away the fear

Of another year like last year
So short of grass an' hay.
This year the calves are heavier
An' gainin' ev'ry day.

They've been weaned 'bout two weeks now.
Tomorrow we'll hit the trail
An' drive them dogies into town
An' try to top the sale.

Hoss, I know that winter's comin'
With wind an' snow an' cold.
I know we both like summer best
Now that we're getting' old.

But fall is mighty pretty...
I reckon it's a bummer
That fall comes ahead of winter
An' not ahead of summer.

We've seen a lot of years, ol' hoss,
An' we both know one thing—
When this winter's finally over
We'll have another spring

With calves...an' foals...an' sunshine...
So jist hold on 'til then...
An' when the springtime gets here
We'll both feel young again.

Fall Calves

Bean Hole Beans

We set up our camp
near Custer Flats Crick.
We'd be there a couple of days.
Cookie parked the wagon in the
shade of some trees.
There was plenty of grass there for
graze.

The cattle was mostly up in the hills
While we was down on the flat.
The grass was tall an' the water was
fresh
An' the cattle was all lookin' fat.

We boys kind of buttered up Cookie
all day,
An' we told him there wasn't a soul
That wouldn't gather the wood an'
handle the spade
If he asked us to dig him a hole.

Cookie just grinned. Then he spit
him some juice.
"Git busy, boys!" We knew what that
means.
We gathered the wood an' we dug
him the hole
While Cookie started the beans.

When the Dutch oven held as much
as it could
An' the wood had all burned down
to coals,
We buried the pot deep in the ashes
An' put the dirt back in the hole.

We slept through the night with
dreams of tomorrow
As the moon climbed over the rim,
An' we thought we could smell,
through four feet of dirt,
Beans bubblin' up to the brim.

Sun-up next day we all was a'saddle,
Gath'rin' cows
from the ridges was play.
We pushed 'em all down to the big
holdin' ground
For the brandin' that was set for next
day.

That night we washed up real good
in the crick,
Though our tails was mostly a
draggin'.
Then with smiles on our faces
we all took our places
A respectable space from the
wagon.

But when Cookie let out his favorite
call—
"Come an' get it or I'll throw it
away!"—
We shore got there quick with our
plates in our hands
For this was a real special day.

Them ol' Bean Hole Beans just can't
never be beat.
Them biscuits was real sourdough,
An' the taters was baked in that same
hand-dug hole
An' the beef had been simmered— real
slow.

Our bellies was full
when we finished our plates
But we somehow found room
for the pie.
Cookie and we-uns had
all earned the best
On that wonderful Fourth of July.

A lot of years now have gone
over the hill.
We're most of us lame, an' some dead,
But that Fourth of July on Custer Flats
Crick
Is a day that is locked in our head.

We no longer ride 'em from sunup 'til
dark
Chasin' them cows from their lair,
But don't think we don't know what
cowboyin's like
Just 'cause there's gray in our hair.

Terry an' Butch and Boots and ol' Lee
An' Gornie and Rocky will do.
Wherever they are, there's one thing we
know—
We once were a heck of a crew.

Bean Hole Beans

Freedom

Once his war whoop ruled the prairies
In a freedom Heaven sent.
Once his voice spoke forth in council
In his tribal government.

Now he lives in faded glory
Of the life he cannot know.
His reservation has confined him
Like the fenced-in buffalo.

Oh, the white man built the fences
And proclaimed his victory,
But the red man and the bison
Both maintain that they are free

For their pride holds forth their greatness
And their history remains
While the royal blood of freedom
Keeps on flowing in their veins.

Subjugation can't be given
If the subject doesn't take,
And freedom lives forever
In the heart that doesn't break.

Freedom

Bringin' 'Em In

We just got the phone call this mornin',
Cousin Eddie's comin' out with his kids.
They're gonna be here a couple of days
An' there's one thing they ain't never hid.

We know that they come to play cowboy—
To saddle up and ride horseback, of course,
So we've adjusted the jobs we was plannin' to do
An' went to get each one a horse.

They live in a city with pavement.
Skyscrapers are the end of their view.
This ranch lets 'em feel like a cowboy for real
An' that's somethin' each young'un should do.

When they leave us late next Sunday ev'nin'
They'll have a new outlook on life.
So that's why I'm bringin' in horses again—
For Eddie, his kids, an' his wife.

To us, a horse is a tool that we use
In our work on this place where we live,
But for two days they're gonna be toys for our kin.
It's a gift that we're happy to give.

Eddie growed up just over that ridge.
He has roots in this hill country land.
He finds here the peace of his youth for himself
An' it helps his three kids understand.

Bringin' 'Em In

73

I Would Go Again to the Mountain

Oh, it's high upon the mountain
Where man's feet have seldom trod
That I'd like to spend an hour
At the footstool of my God.

Yes, it's high upon the mountain
Where the winter blizzards blow
An' even summer sunshine
Leaves the mountain capped in snow.

Where the rocky crags reach skyward
With the clouds around their feet
An' the mountain goat an' bighorn
Are the company you keep.

Though my youth no longer lingers,
An' ol' age has bid me stop,
Still my heart an' mind keep turnin'
To that barren mountain top

Where I've spent those silent hours
Far above man's mortal sod—
An' once more I would sit again
At the footstool of my God.

For I have no friend who's dearer.
I know His love will never stop.
An' someday I will sit with Him
Far above that mountain's top.

Until then we'll walk together.
In His company I'll trod,
But my heart an' mind are yearnin'
For the footstool of my God.

I Would Go Again to the Mountain

75

Ol' Windy

It's not a skyscraper out on the prairie—
Nor a creek or a waterfall,
But if some places didn't have windmills
They couldn't run cattle at all.

A cow'll graze a rough pasture all summer
An' winter on ol' prairie hay,
But a cow just can't live without water
An' they'll drink eight to ten gallons a day.

They'll graze up to a mile from the water
But that's a long way to return,
So it's better to cut that distance in half
An' it don't take cows long to learn.

There's plenty of wind on the prairie,
So a windmill runs kinda cheap
So here's a salute to "Ol' Windy"—
A hand that keeps earnin' its keep.

Ol' Windy

Have You Ever...?

Have you climbed the stormy mountains on their dim an' dusty trails?
Have you dared the highest peaks to seek the sun?
Have you faced the wind an' weather
'Til your skin turns into leather
An' you felt that God above an' you were one?

Have you ridden through the desert on caballos sore of foot?
Have you traveled 'cross the valleys and the plains?
Have you chased the longhorn cattle
'Til your bones would shake an' rattle
An' only God above could know your pains?

Have you braved the river's rapids as they dropped off to the sea?
Have you walked the path the deer made through the breaks?
Have you heard the loon a'callin'
An' the bull moose with his bawlin'?
Have you found the face of God in moonlit lakes?

Have you sat in your log cabin as the howling winds blew by
An' your family huddled close around the fire?
Have you listened to the blizzard
That would freeze a grizzly's gizzard?
Have you known when God was venting forth His ire?

As each age has taught you lessons of this land we love so well,
As you've journey'd all those years upon this sod,
Have you traveled 'cross this nation—
Have you thrilled to the creation—
Do you know the great Creator men call God?

Have You Ever...?

79

The Protector

With hoof as hard a granite
The Protector leads his band.
He an' his free-runnin' mares
Are possessors of this land.

From those mountains to the westward,
To the sandhills down below,
The Protector leads his maidens
Wherever he decides to go.

The wildness in his bearing
Is the wildness in his heart.
They stay alive, this band of his,
Because he does his part.

When another stallion nickers
The Protector answers back.
He'll fight to save his harem—
To keep his band intact.

But now he sees another sight
That's brand new to his brain.
It's trucks an' men an' trailers
Invading his domain.

Last night he visited a ranch
An' stole that good gray mare.
The cowboys plan to get her back
An' two or three to spare.

The Protector watches warily.
Which way is best to run?
The clouds are threat'nin' overhead
As he stands there in the sun.

He doesn't know his days are numbered.
He'll fight on 'til the end.
He still is their Protector,
But he'll not defeat the men

For with horses, trucks an' rifles
His enemy's too good.
The Protector's mares will soon be theirs
An' he'll be coyote food.

Civilization sets the price
The horses now must pay.
Like buffalo an' Indians—
Was it meant to be that way?

Or can we, like The Protector,
Protect our precious land
From thieves an' politicians
An' others not so grand

Who'd take away our freedoms—
Our churches an' our guns—
Our fam'lies an' our money—
Our land an' what it runs?

Thank God our Founding Fathers
Fought to make us free.
Let's not let politicians make
Buzzard bait of you an' me.

The Protector

Cowboy Up, America

When the white man came to the west of our land
He was chasin' the dreams of his soul.
Was it beaver or gold or timber or crops
Or the view that he got from a knoll?

Was it shootin' the buffalo just for his hide
Or gatherin' their bones for potash?
Was it layin' a track for the railroad to use
Or to fight in some Indian/White clash?

Out in the West a man's handshake's his bond.
His word's still accepted as true.
The cowboy, the horse and the old Longhorn cow
Are a part of the red, white an' blue.

Cowboy Up, America

About the Author

Charles E. "Charlie" Hunt of Rapid City, South Dakota, had his first poem published when he was nine years old. Having grown up in the Dakotas, he grew up the "cowboy" way. He ranched and rodeod and has generally been a cowboy until he was old enough to be a cattleman. He and his wife Glorine raise registered Angus cattle. They have four children, three grandchildren and three great-grandchildren.

Although he makes his living as a real estate broker and in writing, he is also an ordained minister serving Big Bend Presbyterian Church in the Black Hills.

He has had articles published in several national and regional magazines and his syndicated weekly column, "Scene from the Saddle" is approaching its twelfth year. His first book, *FOR COWBOYS, CAMPERS AND COMMON FOLK, If you Ain't One of These, Don't Buy It*, sold out after two printings. He has twice represented South Dakota at Elko, Nevada Cowboy Poetry Gathering and has presented his program of Cowboy Poetry in eleven states. Hunt was the first president of the South Dakota Cowboy Poets Association.

Hunt is a member of the Black Hills Angus Association, the American Angus Association, the American Quarter Horse Association, the South Dakota Stock Growers, and a life member of the American Angus Association and the National Rifle Association.

He's also a member of the Western Writers of America, the National Writers Association, the Black Hills Writers Group, The South Dakota Historical Society, the Museum of the Fur Trade, the Westerners and an honorary member of the 50 Years in the Saddle Club in North Dakota.

He's listed in the National Registry of Who's Who and received the Rapid City Area Chamber of Commerce "Aggie of the Year" Award in 1996.

l to r: Leo Giacommetto; Oakley Lamphere;
Kyle Evans; Charlie's "Ranch Foreman" and grandson,
Dustin Kindred; Charlie Hunt; and Lavon Shearer.

Author **CHARLIE HUNT**

About the Artist

Daryl Poulin and his wife Debbie live on an acreage west of Cheyenne, Wyoming, where Daryl is a full time artist. He is well-known in the world of western art and has been commissioned by national and international corporations to create commemorative paintings and prints. These include the official painting for the 75th Anniversary of the Buffalo Bill Cody Stampede in Cody, Wyoming.

Poulin was born and raised in Maine. From there he went to Korea as a member of the army. Upon his return he studied for two years at the Chicago Art Institute. That experience led him to the Portland, Maine, School of Art where he earned a Bachelor of fine Arts degree in graphic design. He made his living that way in Rapid City and in Milwaukee, but he made his life reliving the West and its history through his western paintings.

While riding horseback up in the Shoshones, Poulin found what he'd been looking for for so long. "It was like a rock hit me on top of the head," Poulin says with a grin. "I thought, 'What have I been missing?' I fell in love with the West and knew I wanted to paint it."

Poulin had never painted because he "couldn't find anything I wanted to paint." Suddenly he had found the life he wanted to paint and the life he wanted to live. He soon moved to Cheyenne so he could live it.

As art director of a major Milwaukee advertising agency, Poulin lived surrounded by skyscrapers. Now he lives near Cheyenne, a "town that is still proud to be Western. If you're going to paint Western, you darn sure better live in it," Poulin says. "This isn't just about painting the life, it's about living the life."

Actress Melanie Griffith purchased his first painting and he was off and painting the West. Today his paintings hang in galleries in Wyoming, Colorado, Arizona, South Dakota, and Montana as well as in many private homes and businesses.

With well over 100 paintings completed, Poulin's works have also become limited edition prints and posters and pictures commissioned by international companies.

Daryl Poulin is recognized in the art world as one of the good ones.

Artist **DARYL POULIN**

To order copies of
ALL THE HORSES HE'D RODE:

Please send:

_____copies of *All the Horses He'd Rode* at $49.95 each

TOTAL _____

Nebraska residents add 5% sales tax _____
South Dakota residents add 4% sales tax

Shipping/Handling
   $5.00 for first book
   $1.00 for each additional book _____

TOTAL ENCLOSED _____

Name _____

Address _____

City_____State_____Zip _____

☐ Visa   ☐ MasterCard   ☐ Discover

Credit card number _____Expiration date _____

Dageforde Publishing, Inc.

128 East 13th Street
Crete, NE 68333-2235
1-800-216-8794
or on our secure website at
www.dageforde.com

OLD WEST COMPANIES, INC.
(605) 348-6505   P.O. Box 9106   Rapid City, SD 57709

Old West Publishing Co.

PO Box 9106
Rapid City, SD 57709-9106
605-348-6505
email: owescrow@rapidnet.com